EXTINCT

TYRANNOSAURUS REX

Ben Garrod

Illustrated by Gabriel Ugueto

ZEPHYR

An imprint of Head of Zeus

This is a Zephyr book, first published in the UK in 2021
by Head of Zeus Ltd
This paperback edition first published in the UK in 2023
by Head of Zeus Ltd, part of Bloomsbury Publishing Plc

9 7 5 3 1 2 4 6 8

A catalogue record for this book is available from
the British Library.

ISBN (PB): 9781838935399
ISBN (E): 9781838935405

Typesetting and design by Nicky Borowiec and Catherine Gaffney

Printed and bound in Serbia by Publikum d.o.o.

EXTINCT

IN THIS SERIES BY BEN GARROD AND GABRIEL UGUETO

Hallucigenia

Dunkleosteus

Trilobite

Lisowicia

Tyrannosaurus rex

Megalodon

Thylacine

Hainan gibbon

ALSO BY BEN GARROD

The Chimpanzee and Me

Ultimate Dinosaurs series:

Diplodocus

Triceratops

Spinosaurus

Tyrannosaurus rex

Stegosaurus

Velociraptor

Ankylosaurus (June 2023)

Microraptor (September 2023)

'There is no reason to suppose that our stay here will be any more permanent than that of the dinosaurs.'

David Attenborough

CONTENTS

Introduction   1

† **What is Extinction?**   5

? **Why Do Species Go Extinct?**   11

    ✳ Diseases, Predation and Competition   16

    🐝 Coextinction   20

    Genetic Mixing   22

    🌴 Habitat Destruction   24

    🌡 Climate Change   25

🕐 **Timeline**   28

☠ **Mass Extinctions**   31

🦤 **The End Cretaceous Mass Extinction**   37

    🌡❄ Causes   39

    🌼 Effects   46

🐦 **Ask the Expert**   58

🐦 **Tyrannosaurus rex**   63

   🔍 *Tyrannosaurus rex*: Discovery   64

   🦴 *Tyrannosaurus rex*: Anatomy   70

   🧩 *Tyrannosaurus rex*: Classification   84

   🐦 *Tyrannosaurus rex*: Ecology   90

Glossary   112

INTRODUCTION

For as long as there has been life on Earth, there has been extinction, and given enough time, all species will one day go extinct. Every day, it seems, we hear more and more tragic stories about more and more species being closer to extinction. There are scientists, conservationists, charities, universities, communities and even a few good governments fighting against extinction and trying to save some of our most treasured species and habitats. But, and there is a *but* to this story, extinction has its place in our world and, at the right level and at the right time, it is a perfectly natural occurrence and can even help evolution in some ways.

I am a scientist. It's the very best job in the world. In my work, I look at evolution and I've been lucky enough to spend time with some of the most endangered species on our planet, as well as a few which have already gone extinct. I'm fascinated by the effects extinction has on nature, in the broader sense. But how much do we *really* know about extinction?

If we are to ever stand a chance of saving species from extinction, then first we need to understand it. What is extinction? What causes it? What happens when many species go extinct at once? I want to explore extinction as a biological process and investigate why it can sometimes be a positive thing for evolution, as well as, at times, nature's most destructive force. Let's put it under the microscope and find out everything there is to know.

When a species goes extinct, we place a dagger symbol (†) next to its name when it's listed or mentioned in a scientific manner. So, if you do see the name of a species with a little dagger after it, you'll know why. It's extinct. In this series, I have written about eight fantastic species. Starting with *Hallucigenia* (†), then *Dunkleosteus* (†) and trilobites (†), through to *Lisowicia* (†), *Tyrannosaurus rex* (†) and megalodon (†), before finishing with thylacine (†)

and lastly, the Hainan gibbon. Of these, only the Hainan gibbon does not have a dagger next to its scientific name, meaning it is the only animal we still have a chance of saving from extinction.

Professor Ben Garrod

WHAT IS EXTINCTION?

OFTEN IN BIOLOGY, as is the case with much of science, there are many definitions for a lot of complicated terms. Understanding the essence of extinction, though, is not especially complicated – it is when the species is dead. Not just the individual animal or a large group of animals which are the same, but all animals of that species. When there are no more left alive and the last one dies, then that species is extinct. Lost. Gone forever.

Something I have a lot of trouble with when we talk about extinction is the question, 'So what? Who really cares if a species dies out? What difference does it really make? So what if another type of frog disappears?' The truth is there are people who you'll never convince that it's vitally important we fight against extinction right now. They're frequently the same people who don't believe our climate is rapidly changing, and who argue against so much of modern science. But why *does* it matter if a species disappears?

There's a simple answer and a much more complicated answer. The simple answer is that as humans, we occupy a unique position in the animal kingdom. We understand a great deal. We have the power and the ability to completely shape and control the world around us, and with that comes a duty to protect others within our community, whether

Eurasian lynx

they're our human neighbours in our street or our animal neighbours in forests and reefs and in our gardens.

The second answer is because the natural world is a wondrous interconnected ecosystem, in which there are many examples of species linking to one another. Nature is like a big spider web, connecting billions of organisms with invisible strands, just like a web. If one species is removed, it pulls on another part of that web. If enough species are made extinct, then the whole structure is destroyed.

This idea helps you understand how removing natural predators from an ecosystem could mean that your home gets flooded. There are very few natural predators in the UK nowadays. Wolves and lynx have all been killed, and we trapped, shot and stole eggs from so many birds of prey that their numbers crashed. This gave prey animals, such as rabbits and deer, a huge opportunity. Their populations rose and rose, to the point where they ate so much vegetation, they changed the landscape,

Eurasian wolf

turning habitats dotted with bushes and trees to almost bare environments.

Now, when there is heavy rainfall, the water runs straight down hills rather than soaking into the roots and thicker soil layers created by habitats with lots of trees and bushes. Streams and then rivers flood, which ultimately floods towns, villages and homes along the way. In reality, flooding is a lot more complicated than this, but this little example does help show how removing organisms from an environment can have far-reaching impacts. With so many species of plants, animals, fungi and other life, who knows what catastrophic effect a species going extinct might have.

Extinction has been present since the first life on Earth popped into existence, which must mean that loads *and loads* of species have gone extinct. It's hard to get your head around how many. Scientists predict that as many as 99 per cent of the species that have *ever* lived have gone extinct and if you're wondering how many species that might be, then if their calculations are correct, it means we have already lost an almost unbelievable five billion species from our planet.

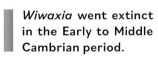

Wiwaxia went extinct in the Early to Middle Cambrian period.

We cannot be certain, because many extinctions stretch back millions (or even hundreds of millions) of years and because there wasn't a scientist standing there with a camera or a notebook, we shall never know about many of these losses. Scientists believe that there may be 10–14 million different species (although some believe this figure might even be as high as one trillion). Of those, only 1.2 million have been documented and recorded in a proper scientific way, meaning we don't know about 90 per cent of life on planet Earth right now.

Here's where it gets a little complicated. Extinction is natural. Even we human beings will go extinct one day. It might sound sad, but that's because you're thinking from the point of view of a person. We are simply one of those 14 million or so species, remember. Usually, a species has about 10 million years or so of evolving, eating, chasing, playing, maybe doing homework, building nests or even going to the moon before it goes extinct and ends up in the history (or even *prehistory*) books. Some species last longer than this, some are around for less time.

WHY DO SPECIES GO EXTINCT?

IMAGINE A HUGE shoal of sardines. Tens of millions of small fish darting left and right, early morning sunlight shimmering off their silvery bodies as they flee the attention of hungry whales, dolphins, gannets, bronze whalers and other sharks. These shoals can be over 1.5km wide and can reach an astonishing 7km from the front to the back of the gathering. They are so big that they look like huge oil slicks from above. There are so many fish that it's easy to forget there are tens of millions of *individuals* in that shoal and that's the key to their success. It's the key to the success for any species.

Despite looking identical, these sardines are unique, each with their own genetic blueprint. These minor differences might give an individual a tiny advantage over others, such as escaping a hungry predator, like this dolphin.

If every one of those sardines were exactly the same, they'd be genetic clones. OK, there would still be differences based on how much each one eats and other things influenced by the environment but at the level of their genes, their DNA would all be the same. But this is not how nature usually works and instead, every single individual is slightly different (even if they do all happen to look the same), as each one has a slightly different DNA *recipe*. It's because of this tiny amount of variation in every individual that species avoid going extinct every day. If something in the environment suddenly changes and makes it much harder to survive, then it has a devastating impact on every individual.

But imagine if the temperature suddenly increases, or the levels of oxygen drop dangerously, or the type of food which is regularly eaten disappears, then those few individuals within that population which are, through random chance, able to tolerate such a fluctuation in temperature or a change in the available oxygen or a switch in available food might stand a slightly higher chance of tolerating that change and surviving. They're

the ones that will pass on their genes and, over time, the whole population will bounce back, able to survive the change. If there isn't enough individuality to survive such a change, or if that change is just too big to survive, then the species is likely to slip into extinction.

There are almost limitless reasons which might lead to extinction but they all have one thing in common. They all focus on a change. These changes can be either in the species' physical environment, such as the actual destruction of a habitat, flooding or drought. The change might be in its 'biological environment', such as the arrival of a new predator or the development of a new deadly disease. If the species does not have enough time to change or simply cannot change, then it will die out and become extinct.

Scientists estimate that on average, a species is likely to exist between one million and 10 million years, before going extinct. Some will last longer and others for only a fraction of that time. There are a variety of general causes that can lead, directly or indirectly, to the extinction of a species or group of species.

DISEASES, PREDATION AND COMPETITION

Diseases are one of those things which are often linked to extinction. Practically every species alive has its own set of diseases and those which it can pick up from other species. One of the most fascinating examples of how a disease can affect a species, almost to the point of extinction, is seen in the Tasmanian devil.

In 1996, it was reported that a newly identified infectious cancer was spreading through the devil populations in Tasmania, passed between devils through biting one another. Devil facial tumour disease affects this famous little carnivorous marsupial, causing painful ulcers around the mouth and tumours on the jaws which eat into the bone. As the disease gets worse, tumours cover the eyes and the devil usually dies from infection or starvation. It kills nearly 100 per cent of those animals affected and, in some areas, 95 per cent of the population was lost. The Tasmanian devil was very nearly made extinct, before conservation work started making progress recently.

Tasmanian devil

In a natural situation, it's very unusual for a predator to cause the total extinction of its prey, because the two are in balance, where both evolve to be better predators or be better at avoiding predators. This delicate relationship can take millions of years to develop and is a good example of what we call coevolution, where the evolution of two species are closely tied together. But when a predator is suddenly introduced to an environment, then the prey has no time to evolve to avoid being eaten.

The brown tree snake is found naturally in parts of Australia, eastern Indonesia, Papua New Guinea and many other islands in the region. However, at some point not long after the end of the Second World War, these snakes were accidentally introduced to Guam, a small island in the western Pacific Ocean. This island had never had snakes on it before, but did have lots of birds, many of which had no predators. The birds were easy targets for the snakes, which bred and bred and bred, and now, bird populations have completely crashed on Guam. Two species found nowhere else on the

Guam flycatcher and brown tree snake

planet, the Guam flycatcher and the Guam rail, are now both extinct in the wild, although a few rail have been bred in captivity. As many as 12 species have been driven to extinction on the island, although some survive elsewhere.

I'm fascinated by the problem of introduced predators, especially those on island ecosystems. Apart from climate change, they're one of the greatest threats to our global biodiversity. In a weird coincidence, just as I was writing about this one particular problem predator today, I read that there was a new twist in the story of the brown tree snake on Guam. Conservationists have started protecting nesting birds by placing smooth metal tubes around trees, to stop the snakes from reaching the nests. They've now discovered a brand new type of behaviour, never seen in snakes before: where the brown tree snake turns its body into a lasso, looping around the smooth cover and edges its way up. Once a predator is introduced into a new environment, there is very often little that can be done to stop the consequences.

Our nearest human relative now is the chimpanzee (and I'm a big fan of them – I even consider one or two my friends) but from an evolutionary perspective, our nearest relatives were the Neanderthals (NEE an-der tharl-z). These amazing people created art, made musical instruments, cared for their sick and elderly and wore jewellery. They thrived for at least 250,000 years, and then, around 40,000 years ago, they sadly disappeared. This is a fascinating area of study and there's still so much being researched, but it's likely that our human cousins went extinct for a combination of reasons, with competition with our own species and climate change being at the top of the list. There are lots of ideas as to how we may have outcompeted these clever, strong people, and although it could have been because we managed better in a changing climate, or had better tools, or better clothes, or even because we domesticated wolves, which helped us hunt better, what actually happened is, for now, a bit of a mystery.

COEXTINCTION

Sometimes, a species evolves alongside another species so closely that when one goes extinct, there is nothing the other can do but go extinct too. This might be a specific parasite depending on a specific host species or a particular pollinating insect needing one species of plant in order to survive. An extreme example of a coextinction is the moa and the Haast's eagle. Moa were huge flightless birds found on New Zealand, with some being as much as 3.6m in height and 230kg in weight.

Hungry Haast eagle chicks feed on moa.

The Haast's eagle was their main predator. When human settlers hunted the last moa into extinction around 600 years ago, the eagles were left with no food and they too went extinct.

GENETIC MIXING

Every species has its own set of genetic data unique to that particular species. It's like the species' recipe. If a little bit of it is changed, then it's a different species, just like a recipe. Sometimes, similar ingredients can be mixed to produce slightly different dishes or to make something completely different. I'm a creature of habit. I like to have beans on toast every day for breakfast. Bread, butter, baked beans, pepper and a splash of my favourite sauce. But if I change one ingredient, the whole meal changes.

In the same way, mixing species can completely change the result, sometimes making one, or even both, of the original species go extinct. The Cuban crocodile is found, as you may have guessed, on Cuba. At a maximum length of around 3.5m, it's smaller than some other species but is an aggressive member of the crocodilian group. It's also 'Critically Endangered', which means it's a step away from extinction. One of the biggest problems facing the Cuban crocodile and the conservationists trying to save it is that it's breeding with the more common American crocodile. Over time, there will still be plenty of American crocodiles left because they have such a large range, but it's possible the Cuban crocodile will disappear and what's left will be a new species, a mixture of the two. This mixing of species is hybridisation and although it isn't a major reason for extinction, it does contribute.

Cuban crocodile

HABITAT DESTRUCTION

When we talk about this cause of extinction, we usually use the phrase 'habitat loss' but we don't lose habitats, we destroy them. Admitting this is a step in the right direction needed to protect many habitats and ecosystems around the world. The saddest thing about habitat destruction is that it means devastation not only for individual organisms but sometimes for entire species. In the UK, a rail line is being built to link two cities. These cities are already linked, but the plan is to make the journey slightly quicker. Shaving a few minutes off a journey and linking parts of the country is important but is it worth the cost to the environment? The UK's largest woodland conservation charity states that 108 ancient woodlands will be damaged, 33 Sites of Special Scientific Interest (meant to receive the highest level of protection in the UK) will be affected and 21 nature reserves will be

Sycamore
seed

completely destroyed. Some of these habitats are classed as 'ancient woodlands', meaning they are hundreds of years old, incredibly important for biodiversity and considered irreplaceable by the government itself. Although they have offered to replant several million young trees, it will take hundreds of years before they're as valuable as the ancient woodlands they're meant to replace. With the project costing around £88 billion, it's an expensive way to destroy unique habitats to make a small difference.

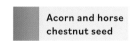

Acorn and horse chestnut seed

CLIMATE CHANGE

Some big things happen really quickly, such as a bolt of lightning or an earthquake. Others take their time, but have an impact as big, or even bigger. The biggest of these threats is climate change. Right now, it sits above mudslides, avalanches, tsunamis and forest fires. Any one of these natural disasters is a terrible threat. But where an avalanche might kill hundreds of animals, a tsunami might mean the end of thousands and forest fires might take millions of lives, the effects of climate change on our planet are hard to imagine. Trillions and trillions of animals, plants and other organisms are at risk, meaning millions of species will be pushed into extinction. As our world grows warmer, our seas become more acidic and ocean levels rise, the need to act has never been greater. It's pretty easy to find species which have already *gone* extinct from climate change. Everything from the mighty *Tyrannosaurus rex* to the towering steppe mammoths have been lost for this reason.

What's even easier to predict is which species are *going* to be in trouble because of climate change, because the answer is simple. Most of them. Unless we act now. The only thing that is more of a threat than climate change is not doing anything about climate change.

There will be people – politicians, celebrities, even scientists – who tell you climate change doesn't exist or that it's natural and we don't need to act. As a young scientist, do you listen to the evidence presented from thousands of different experts in hundreds of different reports, or do you believe someone who wants to convince you because they want to make money, or gain power, or because they simply don't understand how science, and the processes scientists use, work? You decide.

The dodo went extinct in 1681.

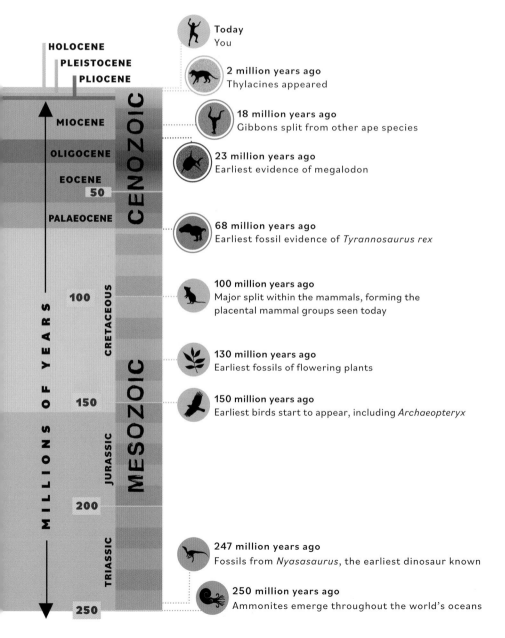

HOLOCENE
PLEISTOCENE
PLIOCENE

CENOZOIC

MIOCENE

OLIGOCENE

EOCENE
50

PALAEOCENE

100

CRETACEOUS

150

MESOZOIC

JURASSIC

200

TRIASSIC

250

MILLIONS OF YEARS

Today
You

2 million years ago
Thylacines appeared

18 million years ago
Gibbons split from other ape species

23 million years ago
Earliest evidence of megalodon

68 million years ago
Earliest fossil evidence of *Tyrannosaurus rex*

100 million years ago
Major split within the mammals, forming the placental mammal groups seen today

130 million years ago
Earliest fossils of flowering plants

150 million years ago
Earliest birds start to appear, including *Archaeopteryx*

247 million years ago
Fossils from *Nyasasaurus*, the earliest dinosaur known

250 million years ago
Ammonites emerge throughout the world's oceans

MILLIONS OF YEARS

PERMIAN

300

CARBONIFEROUS

350

DEVONIAN

400

SILURIAN

450

ORDOVICIAN

500

CAMBRIAN

PALAEOZOIC

PROTEROZOIC

ARCHEAN

300 million years ago
Lisowicia first appeared

320 million years ago
'Mammal-like reptiles', including *Dimetrodon*, evolve

340 million years ago
Earliest amphibians

382 million years ago
Earliest evidence of *Dunkleosteus*

385 million years ago
Oldest fossilised tree

400 million years ago
Earliest fossils of insects

Some of the dates for earliest fossils are estimates based on our best understanding right now. They are not always perfect and the more evidence we collect, the more certain we can be and the more accurate these dates will eventually become.

500 million years ago
Fossil evidence from *Hallucigenia*

520 million years ago
Earliest vertebrates emerged (and may have looked like small eels)

530 million years ago
Earliest fossils of trilobites

680 million years ago
Earliest ancestors of jellyfish and their relatives

2.15 billion years ago
Earliest evidence of bacteria

3 billion years ago
Earliest evidence of viruses

MASS EXTINCTIONS

RIGHT NOW, somewhere in the world, something, for some reason, will be going extinct, hopefully due to natural causes. In the same way that the evolution and appearance of a species is completely natural, so too is the constant loss of species. Species come and go in a cycle, a bit like tides moving back and forth or the changing of the seasons.

Extinction is unavoidable and goes on at a fairly predictable rate wherever life exists. We call this background extinction: constant, low-level extinction which doesn't cause major problems on a wider scale,

Hallucigenia

other than for the species going extinct, that is. These 'everyday extinctions' go mostly unnoticed by the majority of us. This all changes when we talk about a mass extinction.

For the purposes of my books, we are going to treat a mass extinction as the worldwide loss of around 75 per cent (or more) of species, over a short space of 'geological' time. If you're wondering how short 'a short space of geological time' is, then let's say it has to be under three million years. This might sound a very long time, but remember Earth is around four and a half *billion* years old.

Mass extinctions, as you might expect, involve loss of life on an enormous scale, either across

Dunkleosteus

Trilobite

a large number of species or groups, or across a significant part of the planet, or both. In a mass extinction event, the rate of species being lost is greater than the rate by which species are evolving. Imagine you're slowly filling a bucket with water, but there's a big hole in its side; over time, that bucket will still become empty.

Over the last 500 million years or so, the Earth has experienced multiple mass extinctions, ranging from five to as many as 20, depending on what definitions (and there are a number of different ones) scientists use. In the worst of these mass extinction events, over 90 per cent of life on Earth has been wiped out, and in terms of life recovering to a level from before the event, it may take at least 10 million years for biodiversity levels to return to what they once were.

Lisowicia

Megalodon

Some mass extinctions, like the one caused by the asteroid 66 million years ago at the end of the Cretaceous period, are pretty quick, while others spread across hundreds of thousands of years to take full effect.

When we talk about mass extinctions, most scientists agree there are five classic mass extinctions, with the earliest occurring around 450 million years ago and the most recent 66 million years ago. In addition to these famous five mass extinctions, another was identified recently, which struck around 2.5 million years ago.

Now, many scientists say we are entering (or even in) the sixth mass extinction event, but this is something which needs to be looked at closely

Thylacine

for two reasons. First, I've mentioned the recently identified mass extinction which occurred just over two million years ago, which would make that the sixth mass extinction and the current global extinction event would be the seventh, in fact. Second, as we'll see later in the series, it's really hard to say exactly when most mass extinctions start, so, as bad as it is right now, we may not even be in one yet.

Hainan gibbon

Throughout the series, we're going to look at the five classic mass extinctions, the newly discovered mass extinction and the current extinction event which is being triggered by us. Finally, we'll look at how scientists and conservationists are tackling the threat of extinction and explore what can be done.

THE END CRETACEOUS MASS EXTINCTION

BAD DAYS HAPPEN to us all. Yes, some are much worse than others; turning up at school and discovering there's an unexpected test, or stubbing your toe when you trip over your dog. But your terrible day is nothing like one particular day, tens of millions of years ago, that changed every single life on the planet. A whopping 75 per cent of that life was ended because of this *really* bad day. As far as bad days go, this was the BIG one.

What started off as a speck high in the sky would, in a matter of seconds, have revealed itself to be an enormous natural missile from space, travelling at tens of thousands of kilometres an hour, on a collision course with Earth. In a stroke of massively bad luck, it was due to strike one of the few places on the planet where it would cause maximum devastation. The short- and long-term effects of this famous event changed the global climate in days and helped shape all life on Earth for millions of years to come. It might even be responsible for you sitting and reading this sentence now.

When

This famous mass extinction formed the line between the Cretaceous period and the Paleogene. Although for a long time it was thought to have occurred 65 million years ago, we now believe it happened 66 million years ago.

CAUSES

It might be the most famous ever but it may surprise you to discover that the cause of the End Cretaceous mass extinction has been constantly debated. Even now, a few questions remain as to what really caused the end of the dinosaurs. Well, most of the dinosaurs. On one side of the debate is the story many of us know – a giant asteroid struck the planet and caused global devastation. On the other, the idea of a series of volcanic eruptions which affected the climate and changed the sea levels around the planet. As is often the case with science, the story is complicated and we have to look at all the available evidence before we reach conclusions.

There is a lot to support the volcanic theory in the fossil record. Over 76 million years ago, in what is now India, a huge lava field of volcanoes, fiery lakes and burning rivers raged for over a million years. This huge volcanic landscape is known as the Deccan Traps and the destruction it caused occurred over numerous episodes of intense activity. During this volcanic activity, vast quantities of different greenhouse gases capable of changing the global climate,

In the seconds following the asteroid strike, rock was pushed up with tremendous force, forming a temporary mountain ring higher than the Himalayas, before crashing down again. The local devastation would have been unimaginable.

including carbon dioxide and sulphur dioxide, were released into the atmosphere. Some scientists believe that as a result of this the average surface temperature on Earth may have increased, or even dropped, by as much as 2°C. This may not sound that much, but would be enough to kill many species and groups of species.

When we look at the evidence, it appears that although this volcanic activity was pretty bad news, it was nowhere near bad enough to cause the devastation we see at the end of the Cretaceous period. Scientists found there was no link between the different levels of activity while the Deccan Traps were active and changes in the global climate, meaning all that exploding and flowing lava wasn't responsible.

Dinosaur fossils have been found across the area of the Deccan Traps and throughout the period of the Traps being active. This shows that the volcanic environment can't have been responsible for killing all the dinosaurs on the planet, if it couldn't even kill those living in and around the Deccan Traps themselves.

It's hard not to jump ahead now and shout 'but we know it was the asteroid'. But, like any good scientist, you should always ask, 'where's the proof?' and 'where's the evidence?' It was in the late 1970s that the asteroid was first blamed for the loss of the dinosaurs but scientists were missing one rather important thing. Evidence! That evidence was uncovered when, in 1980, a team of geologists, physicists and chemists identified a very thin layer of metal sediment around much of the Earth. This rare metal was iridium and the team found that it was concentrated in the layer that marked the end of the Cretaceous period perfectly. They also found that the iridium in this layer was up to 160 times more concentrated than other layers they looked at. Iridium doesn't form on our planet. It comes from outer space so the only thing which could explain the layer of iridium around our planet is that an asteroid struck Earth 66 million years ago and left a tell-tale iridium trace of its origins.

The last piece of the great 'whodunnit' Cretaceous mass extinction jigsaw came when a 180km-wide impact crater was found off the northern coast of Mexico in the early 1990s. It was named the Chicxulub (chiks-U-lub) crater and proved that an asteroid was the culprit for the most famous of our planet's mass extinctions. When the layer of iridium and the formation of the crater were aged at 66 million years old, and lined up with the fossil record, which showed that all the big prehistoric marine reptiles, the pterosaurs and the dinosaurs also disappeared around 66 million years ago, scientist were left in no doubt that a huge asteroid was responsible.

The crater was about 20km deep and nearly 200km wide. To create a crater this size, scientists estimated that the asteroid must have had a diameter of at least 10km. Further investigation concluded that at the time of its impact, this asteroid was travelling at a staggering 20km a second. This means it was flying towards the planet at 72,000km per hour. In those same 60 minutes, the asteroid could almost have travelled twice round Earth's circumference, which would take a plane at least 100 hours non-stop (and in reality probably a lot longer).

If you're thinking this was the worst-case scenario, you would *almost* be right, but there were two other important things that made this already-terrible natural disaster a global catastrophe which would affect the planet for the next 66 million years. First, the asteroid struck at a really unfortunate location. If you randomly selected three different points on Earth and dug down, there's a good chance you would encounter one of three different types of rocks and minerals. One is gypsum (jip-sum), a white mineral used in everything from making paper and fertiliser, to building materials such as plaster of Paris and cement. When vaporised, due to an explosion or maybe by the catastrophic impact from a huge asteroid, for example, gypsum releases sulphur. Sulphur mixed with water, such as moisture in the atmosphere, creates sulphuric acid, which, in plain terms, is not a good thing to release into the atmosphere in sudden and huge quantities. And if it seems it was bad luck that the asteroid struck where it did, it's even worse when you realise that Chicxulub is part of just 13 per cent of the Earth's surface where there is enough gypsum to produce such a globally devastating impact. This means that if you randomly picked 100 other possible impact sites for that fateful asteroid strike 66 million years ago, there was almost a 90 per cent chance everything would have been fine and that there wouldn't be a mass extinction.

The second thing which made the terrible event even worse is the angle of the asteroid strike. It was just one of the 25 per cent of asteroids which strike our planet at an angle of around 60 degrees, and in doing so created the most devastating impact possible. We even know it travelled from a northeasterly direction, from where northern Europe is now, before hitting the shallow sea just above Mexico. When all these factors are combined – a large asteroid travelling at a phenomenal speed, striking at the worst possible angle in one of the most unfortunate places on the planet, then you have the recipe for a truly horrifying chain of events.

EFFECTS 🔆75

In 2016, I travelled to a huge, four-legged drilling rig standing in the shallow sea, off the northern coast of Mexico. The water was clear and warm and the sky was bright blue. I was lucky enough to spend time meeting the scientists who were drilling hundreds of metres into the seabed to remove a thin sample of rock, nearly a kilometre long, to see what happened when the asteroid struck, and what the effects were immediately afterwards. I was standing on a mobile marine laboratory in the middle of the sea over the very centre of the Chicxulub crater... it was a geeky dream come true.

A team of scientists had come from universities around the world to investigate building on earlier research and studies. When a 10km-wide asteroid crashes into the Earth at 72,000km per hour, it's pretty obvious that a lot of energy is going to be released. Scientists have estimated that the asteroid would have released more than a billion times the energy of an atomic bomb. This would have had an instant impact. The combination of immense heat and the huge shockwave caused by the impact would have liquified the rock at the impact site and caused the immediate formation of a gigantic mountain range made from granite, rising from the crater, which completely collapsed again minutes later.

The asteroid strike would have generated a terrifying wave of heat which was so hot, scientists have estimated you would have been able to feel it from around 1,500km away. To give you an idea, if it happened in London, you'd be able to feel the impact in Madrid, in

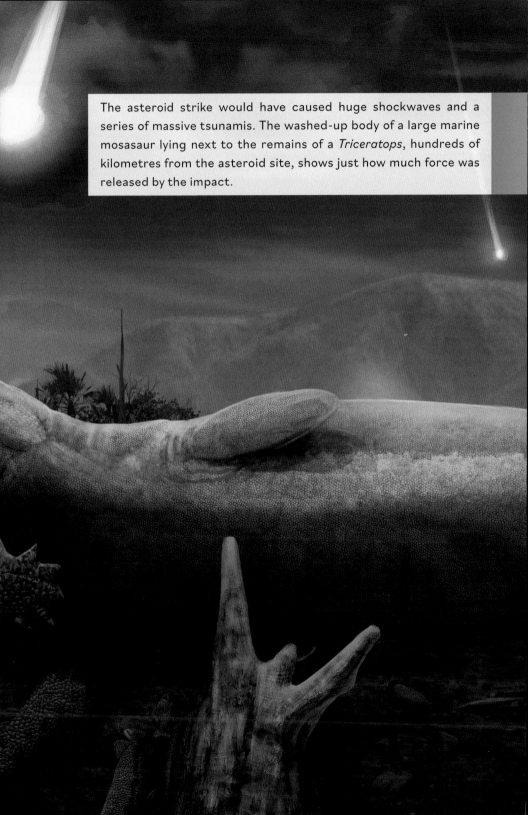

The asteroid strike would have caused huge shockwaves and a series of massive tsunamis. The washed-up body of a large marine mosasaur lying next to the remains of a *Triceratops*, hundreds of kilometres from the asteroid site, shows just how much force was released by the impact.

Spain. It would have killed millions of plants and animals and started thousands and thousands of wildfires, rapidly burning habitats for hundreds of kilometres in every direction. When the mountain range at the impact site collapsed, unimaginably large tsunamis were created at Chicxulub before rolling out across the world's oceans. We have evidence of this in sites where areas which had been burned were left with a layer of sand and stranded marine life, from the tsunamis.

A wall of fiery death, liquified rock, temporary mountains which then collapse, and deadly tsunamis were only the start. When the asteroid struck, it left a huge crater, and millions of tonnes of rock that had to go somewhere. The impact and energy of the asteroid powdered and vaporised the rock, sending it into the atmosphere. The 60-degree angle of the asteroid strike was also the most effective in terms of maximum volume of debris ejected from the crater. A strike at almost any other angle would not have caused as much to be spewed into the atmosphere. Because so much gypsum at the impact site ended up in the atmosphere too, it mixed with moisture in the air to form sulphuric acid, which very quickly fell as lethal acid rain. This led to a rapid increase

in ocean acidity around
the planet, devastating
reef ecosystems and killing
species with shells or exoskeletons
made from calcium carbonate, which
dissolved in the more acidic waters.

Following the impact, debris from the crater was thrown high into the atmosphere, and began to drift back down to Earth. There is some debate about what happened next, but some scientists believe this barrier of ash and soot and vaporised rock would have prevented heat from escaping and would have created a blanket of intense heat, like a planet-sized pizza oven, literally cooking organisms unable to hide. Some research suggests that nearly every terrestrial habitat burned in the hours following the asteroid strike, but we need more evidence to be certain.

After the extreme heat died away, the oceans calmed and the wildfires were put out, the next, and most devastating, stage began. Millions of tonnes of dust, ash, soot and vaporised rock hung in the air, like a dark global cloud. And there it stayed for a while, reducing the amount of sunlight which was able to reach Earth. This would have had two devastating impacts: it would have cooled the planet and prevented plants from properly photosynthesizing.

We don't know what percentage of the sunlight was blocked out, so scientists have investigated the effects of several different scenarios, ranging from a 5 per cent drop to a massive 20 per cent drop, although it was likely to be in the region of 15 per cent. If the light levels dropped by just 5 per cent, the planet would have cooled by 9.7°C, but a 20 per cent drop would have meant the average surface temperature on Earth plummeted by an incredible 66.8°C, plunging us into what some scientists call an 'impact winter'.

The *only* piece of good news (and it's not a huge help) is that the volcanic activity from the Deccan Traps would have added so much carbon dioxide to the atmosphere before the asteroid strike, that it would have offset the dramatic temperature decrease caused by the impact winter, and warmed the atmosphere by nearly 9°C. That would have been great if the planet had cooled by a similar amount, but less ideal if it had dropped by 66.8°C.

The reduced sunlight would have caused the rainfall levels to decrease within months of the impact. A 5 per cent drop would have meant rainfall fell by 14 per cent, whereas a 20 per cent drop would have caused levels to plummet by as much as 95 per cent, turning most of Earth into a dry, icy planet. It's a safe estimate to say the effect was somewhere between these two boundaries and that the level of sunlight reaching the surface of the Earth may have dropped for about 12 months, leading to a 35-degree drop in temperature. This lasted for between three and 15 years after the asteroid impact, and it took as many as 30 years for the Earth to return to the conditions from before the asteroid struck.

In the End Cretaceous mass extinction, 75 per cent of life on the planet was made extinct. It's easy to imagine the asteroid strike was so terrible that absolutely *everything* died in those first few minutes or in the hours which followed, but actually, it took thousands of years for the mass extinction to take full effect.

Although there is some evidence that the biodiversity of dinosaurs was declining in the time leading up to the asteroid strike, other studies conclude they were thriving. Either way, it was not the case that dinosaurs were already heading towards extinction. After the asteroid struck, some species were lost as an immediate result, as the environmental effects built, but the majority were affected much later. Some predictions estimate the mass extinction was in full swing around 32,000 years after the actual asteroid strike.

Quetzalcoatlus, a pterosaur

The most famous losers were the dinosaurs, with some of the most recognisable prehistoric superstars, such as *Triceratops* and *Tyrannosaurus rex*, disappearing forever. It's not actually fair to say the dinosaurs went extinct. They sort of did, but they sort of didn't. Because not *all*

Morturneria, a plesiosaur

Prognathodon,
a mosasaur

the dinosaurs died out as a result of the asteroid.

One group of dinosaurs survived, thrived and continued to do pretty well for the next 66 million years. This group is the birds, which *are* classed as dinosaurs and evolved from the two-legged, mostly carnivorous theropod dinosaurs which included *Velociraptor* (vel oss-EE rap-tor), *Sinornithosaurus* (SII-norn ith-O sor-us), *Spinosaurus* (SPY-no sor-us) and of course *Tyrannosaurus*. So when we say the dinosaurs died out, what we really mean is that the *non-avian* dinosaurs (dinosaurs and groups of dinosaurs which didn't evolve into birds) died out. As well as the majority of dinosaurs, the End Cretaceous mass extinction killed off many mammals, reptiles, insects and plants.

Many species of fish, including lots of sharks, and numerous molluscs, with all the ammonites and belemnites, disappeared. Although a few different marine turtles and some crocodiles and their relatives made it through, nothing bigger than 25kg, about the size of a medium-sized dog or a European beaver, survived the mass extinction. At the site of the crater itself, scientists found evidence that a rich marine ecosystem had returned within 30,000 years, which sounds a long time, but is the blink of an eye in terms of evolution and geology. After one million years, the oceans were once again healthy.

A really interesting aspect of any mass extinction, and especially this one, where so much happened so quickly, is how certain groups survived the disaster. Although some success will be due

Tethydraco,
a pterosaur

to the ability of a particular species to tolerate drastic changes in temperature, their survival also depends on what we call refugia (REE FOO-JEE-a), or little pockets of habitats where the conditions are better or more constant. These safe zones can shelter organisms from the death and destruction going on around them. After the asteroid struck, deep lakes and rivers, deep valleys, coastal environments and many habitats in the tropics would have been possible refugia, allowing some lucky groups to survive the asteroid and its effects.

This is the most famous mass extinction, marking not only the end of the Cretaceous period but also the entire Mesozoic era, which spanned 186 million years across the Triassic, the Jurassic and the Cretaceous periods.

This point, 66 million years ago, also marked the beginning of the Cenozoic era, which continues today.

Hydrotherosaurus, a plesiosaur

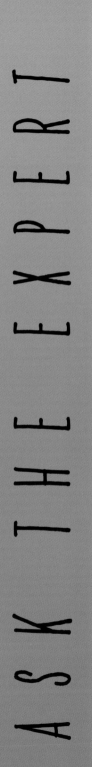

Riley Black is the author of *The Last Days of the Dinosaurs*, *My Beloved Brontosaurus*, and other fossil books. She's an amateur palaeontologist and has joined museum and university field crews from Saskatchewan to Mexico, searching for fossils from the beginning of the Age of Dinosaurs to the Ice Age. She lives in Salt Lake City, Utah.

What is a mass extinction?

Of all the species that have ever evolved, lived and thrived on Earth, 99 per cent are extinct. In fact, extinction is just a part of life's big picture, a counterpoint to the evolution of new species. Sometimes a species vanishes entirely. Other times a species seems to disappear because it has evolved into a different form, connected along life's great thread.

But there have been times when many, many species have vanished within a short amount of time. Palaeontologists call these mass extinctions.

There is no single, standard definition for what qualifies as a mass extinction. All the same, the five major mass extinctions that palaeontologists traditionally recognise are marked by about 75 per cent or more of known fossil species becoming extinct within a window of about two million years.

Some of these extinction events were extremely rapid – during the disaster at the end of the Cretaceous, 66 million years ago, about three-quarters of known species became extinct in a matter of hours to years, including all the non-bird dinosaurs. At the end of the Permian, 251 million years ago, on the other hand, the changes took much longer, to the point that some experts debate whether the signal represents one mass extinction or two.

What makes mass extinctions so important, though, is what happens after. Mass extinctions shake up Earth's habitats, from the seas to the skies. The animals that survive set the stage for the next major flowering of evolution.

ASK THE EXPERT 🦖 61

The mass extinction at the end of the Permian toppled the protomammals from their influential spot and allowed the faster-reproducing reptiles to thrive. Then, at the end of the Cretaceous, the disappearance of the non-avian dinosaurs and many mammal lineages allowed the ancestors of today's placental mammals to thrive.

Despite the catastrophic nature of these events, life has always found a way in the aftermath.

TYRANNOSAURUS REX

WE LIVE IN a world where, for lots of people, being famous is amazing and many of us have a favourite celebrity. Think of your favourite. Maybe a singer, an athlete or TV show presenter. How much do you know about them? Where did they grow up? What's their favourite breakfast? How do they like to relax? I'm guessing that unless you're some sort of megafan, you won't be able to answer many questions about your top celeb. We don't know that much about them and we end up liking them because they seem to be cool, or because other people like them or because... well, just because. And here's my point. *Tyrannosaurus rex* is the biggest celebrity in the fossil record. Before there were global superstars singing in stadiums and playing sports in front of millions, *T. rex* had already become the first megastar. Instantly recognisable, this is the one dinosaur known by adults and children alike. It can be identified in almost any country in any language and we all know something about this famous predator, even if it's just something like it had tiny arms and lots of big teeth. If *T. rex* is going to remain the favourite prehistoric predator for so many of us, we should find out as much as possible about this ultimate Cretaceous celebrity. So, where did *T. rex* grow up? What was their favourite breakfast? How did they like to relax?

DISCOVERY

It seems possible that for as long as our species has been around, we have been fascinated by fossils. Although we don't have written records going all the way back into our own species' past, we know that the ancient Romans and Greeks collected and displayed fossils, but believed them to be from giant people. Fossils in China were thought to be from dragons or gods, and many indigenous communities around the world interpreted fossilised bones and footprints as belonging to fantastic mythical beasts. So although we have been aware of fossils and collected them for thousands of years, if not more, it is only much more recently that we began to look at fossils, and the animals and plants which created them, with a more scientific approach.

The first dinosaur was scientifically named in 1824, by looking at the bones and anatomy and describing the animal based on the evidence available. This animal was *Megalosaurus* (meg-a-LO sor-us) and was described by William Buckland, a geology professor at the University of Oxford, in the UK. Fossilised bones from a similar dinosaur had been found over 200 years earlier but were mistakenly thought to come from huge Roman war elephants. It was nearly 20 years later, in 1842, that another early palaeontologist, Richard Owen, first used the group name 'dinosaur'. So, when the teeth from a *Tyrannosaurus rex* were found in Colorado, USA, in 1874, it was only a few years after we had started studying the newly named group and didn't know much about them. These teeth were not recognised for what they were and over the next few years, they and a bunch of other finds were wrongly identified. We would have to wait a while longer before *Tyrannosaurus rex* was ready to meet the world once again. In the 1890s, fossil bones from its body were incorrectly identified by another famous early fossil hunter, Edward Cope, who thought they were from a relative of the *Triceratops* horned dinosaurs.

Then, in Wyoming in 1900, a group of fossil hunters led by Barnum Brown (known also as 'Mr Bones'), a palaeontologist and curator at the American Museum of Natural History, found the first semi-complete *T. rex* skeleton.

Another find of 34 bones was made in Montana in 1902. In 1905, this magnificent predator was given the name *Tyrannosaurus rex*, from the Greek words *tyrannos*, for 'tyrant', *sauros*, for 'lizard', and from the Latin word *rex*, which translates as 'king'. The name 'tyrant lizard king' meant that nobody would be in any doubt about how impressive *T. rex* really was.

Now, there are many *T. rex* specimens in museums and other collections around the world and discoveries are being made all the time. There are so many great specimens, some with nearly complete skeletons, that they have become quite famous and been given their own names.

The best known of these is Sue. Every fossil specimen that is properly recorded has a unique code. It's why all good fossil discoveries belong in a museum. It means different scientists can identify the right specimen when they study it, to either challenge ideas or develop previous studies. We can't just call this impressive specimen Sue, so its unique code is FMNH PR 2081. This is the oldest, largest and most complete *T. rex* skeleton discovered so far and around 85 per cent has been recovered. Sue was named after amateur palaeontologist Sue Hendrickson who made the discovery in 1990. The fossils were found in the Hell Creek Formation in South Dakota and after an unbelievable 25,000 work hours, the bones were cleaned, the extra rock was removed and they were ready for study.

Another famous *T. rex* is Stan (BHI 3033), named after another amateur palaeontologist, Stan Sacrison. Stan (the dinosaur)

Sue

Stan

was also discovered in the Hell Creek Formation, in 1992. With 199 bones found, about 70 per cent of the skeleton, this makes Stan the second most complete *T. rex* yet found. The third of the famous *T. rex* trio is Scotty (RSM P2523.8).

Scotty was discovered in 1991 in Saskatchewan, Canada, by a high school teacher called Robert Gebhardt, who was with a group of palaeontologists to learn about the processes involved in digging up dinosaurs. Stan's fossils were set within very hard sandstone, where the presence of lots of iron meant it was so difficult to clean the bones, a team spent 20 years preparing them. Now, there is still some disagreement over which *T. rex* was the biggest, Sue or Scotty.

Scotty

ANATOMY

Because *Tyrannosaurus rex* is probably the most easily recognisable dinosaur in the world, you might think we would know pretty much everything about its appearance and anatomy. This could not be further from the truth, as over the last few years, *T. rex* has been given one of the most radical makeovers in palaeontology. What started off resembling a giant, angry lizard standing upright with its tail resting on the ground, weedy little downward-facing arms and green scaly skin has been transformed into a sleeker and more well-balanced predator. Its head is closer to the ground, tail lifted much higher and arms face inwards. Most surprising of all maybe is that like many animals to come in the millions of

Then

Now

years after it, there is every chance *T. rex* was feathered, at least over parts of its body.

Like other tyrannosaurids (TIE-ranno sor-idz), which included its ancestors and other closely related dinosaurs, *T. rex* was bipedal – it walked on two legs. It was a carnivore and had a massive skull for its overall body size. It was the largest terrestrial carnivore and, as far as we are aware, had the greatest bite force of any terrestrial animal.

The biggest *T. rex* skull so far recorded is 152cm long. You might want to measure that against your height for comparison. It had to serve lots of different functions and its size and shape reflects that. Regardless of size, some dinosaur skulls were sleek, others were bulky. The *T. rex* skull was definitely in the bulky category, as it needed to be strong enough to house lots of big teeth and to rip its unfortunate prey apart. But this risked the skull and the whole front half of the body being too heavy and unbalanced.

To make sure this wasn't a problem, the skull had two evolutionary adaptations. Rather than being solid and dense, a lot of the bone had a honeycomb structure, so was air-filled and lighter. This pneumatised (NEW-ma TIE-zd) bone was still very strong, as it had lots of little internal struts and supports, but crucially contributed to reducing a lot of the weight in the head.

The skull also had a lot of big holes in it, which again helped reduce the amount of weight in the head. The structure of these fenestrae (fen-ess TRAY), which means 'windows', would actually have helped strengthen the skull. When looking at a *T. rex* skull from above, you notice that it resembles a big wedge, getting narrower as you move towards the nose – the perfect adaptation for a predator needing good vision. Many prey animals, such as sheep and deer, have eyes on the sides of their skulls, meaning each eye has a large but separate field of view, with very little overlap. Predators, on the other hand, such as wolves and cats, have eyes closer together, on the front of their skulls. Overall, the field of vision might be smaller but, importantly, there is a lot of overlap between what the two eyes can see and it's this overlap zone which gives an animal 3D, or binocular, vision. Whereas prey needs to see as much as possible to spot danger, a predator needs to hunt accurately and having 3D vision allows it to pinpoint its targets more accurately. The shape of the skull and the position of the eyes meant that *T. rex* would have had good 3D vision, enabling it to hunt its prey successfully.

Some of the skull bones, not usually fused in other dinosaurs, were joined in *T. rex*, giving its skull extra strength. This added to the small but important change in the shape of the snout.

Rather than being v-shaped when seen from above or below, the snout and lower jaw of *T. rex* was more u-shaped, which gave it a wider area to anchor its teeth as well as reinforcing the whole structure. For such a big and powerful beast, *T. rex* relied on many small, but nonetheless important, differences to allow it to be the ultimate prehistoric predator.

There would have been lots of reasons not to want to bump into a hungry *T. rex* (or even one that wasn't hungry) but its teeth would probably be at the top of my list. These teeth are often described as banana-like, but this strange mental image doesn't give them the credit they deserve. An adult *T. rex* had 50–60 teeth, which were shaped like, yes, serrated bananas. In cross-section each is D-shaped, curves backwards and has ridges along the back edge, which help increase the strength of the tooth and would have stopped it snapping when biting prey. Like sharks, the teeth were regularly replaced, giving the dinosaur a constant supply of strong, sharp teeth, every nine to 16 months. The teeth in the upper jaw were mostly larger than those in the lower jaw, and varied in shape depending on where they were. The largest teeth could reach 30.5cm in length, but this includes the tooth root, which sat below the gum and wouldn't have been visible.

We should probably talk about *those* arms, shouldn't we? *T. rex* has faced so much teasing and ridicule over its forelimbs. There seems to be a commonly held feeling that in comparison to its big body and huge teeth, the arms were weak, puny and a little funny. But, as with so much about *T. rex*, the truth behind the legend is much more interesting. Despite being called useless and even rubbish, each forelimb was a metre long, and in terms of strength, at the elbow joint, the *T. rex* forelimb was, according to some estimates, able to hold a force of up to 322kg. Even an adult human working out will only ever be able to lift up to 128kg. The moral of this story is that you'd never have beaten a *T. rex* in an arm wrestle.

At the end of each forelimb were two long claws, after the third was lost through evolution and adaptation. It appears that having two claws gave *T. rex* 50 per cent more power than a three-clawed forelimb. Having two powerful claws and a shoulder girdle which was tucked away under the skin and was longer than the rest of their one-metre arm meant that, in theory, the forelimb was capable of being a powerful slashing weapon.

This is an idea most people believe, but when we look from a more scientific perspective, there is evidence for and against the various uses of these short, sharp-clawed limbs. Maybe they were used for dealing with prey close up, such as tearing into unfortunate hadrosaurs. Although 10cm-long claws would have been useful to slash metre-long injuries, it seems likely that if you already have a huge head with huge, sharp teeth, by the time any animal was close enough to your claws, the

damage would already have been done. The claws may have aided younger tyrannosaurs when hunting, but they became less important as they matured and their skull became so large.

Possibly the forelimbs were used to interact with other tyrannosaurs when they fought, or in courtship and mating behaviour. A less obvious use is that they served as biological anchors. In order to function, muscles need to be attached to bone and there is a limit to how much or how many muscles can attach to any one bone. By having a load of extra bone in the chest and shoulder, at the top of the forelimb, a lot more extra muscle from the neck would be able to be anchored, giving *T. rex* a stronger neck and a much greater bite force. We might never know for sure the exact use of these famous forelimbs, but it's likely that they performed a combination of some or all of these roles.

When I first fell in love with dinosaurs, *T. rex* was at the top of my list. It was the ultimate killing machine, because every book, every film and every toy presented *T. rex* as a big, green, scaly, reptilian predator. Now, when I meet young dinosaur enthusiasts and future palaeontologists, they are well aware that many theropod dinosaurs were at least partially feathered. I can still remember the first time I saw a dinosaur shown with feathers and it blew my mind, but at the same time made so much sense. Now we know that some dinosaurs were brightly coloured and others had bold patterned feathers like many birds alive today, but when we talk about whether *T. rex* itself was feathered, we once again find ourselves in the middle of an ongoing disagreement. Some researchers believe *T. rex* was not feathered at all. Others believe they would have been partly covered with feathers.

Just so you know, I'm on the side of the feathers in this argument. So far, there is no direct evidence of fossils from *T. rex* showing feathers and, in fact, some fossils have been found which show parts of the neck, hip and tail all had scales. But there's a famous quote which may (or may not) have been first said by a very cool scientist I once interviewed. The phrase 'the absence of evidence is not the evidence of absence' means just because we haven't found something, doesn't mean it doesn't exist.

When you look at the *T. rex* family tree, there is fossil evidence for both early members of the group and also large tyrannosaur relatives having feathers. The small-bodied *Dilong* (DEE-long) and the much larger *Yutyrannus* (YOO TY-ran-us) were both from China in the early Cretaceous, around 50 million years before *T. rex* stalked the planet. Both have been found to have had feathering across part of their bodies. Although *T. rex* lived much later and in a different part of the world, it closely shared its genetic make-up with these predators and when we are talking about something which is established along an evolutionary line, it doesn't usually suddenly disappear in a related species. It's often too hard for evolution to reverse something big like this. As we make more discoveries, maybe we'll know once and for all.

If you're worried that *T. rex* looked like some sort of feathered predatory prehistoric pigeon, then don't be. It was still every bit the legendary killer we all know and love, and it was huge. The biggest fossils discovered indicate that *T. rex* reached a length of

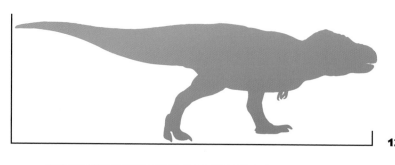

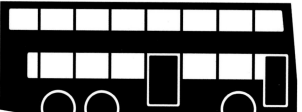

12.3m

12.3m (although Sue may have been 50cm longer). At the highest point of the hip, which is a standard way to measure many animals, both extinct and extant, they measured up to 3.96m from the ground. *T. rex* weighed between 8.4 tonnes and 14 tonnes – the massive skull alone weighed as much as 272kg, which is the equivalent of more than three adult humans. If you're having trouble imagining just how big and heavy *T. rex* was, it was longer and probably heavier than a double-decker London bus.

When I think about dinosaurs, I visualise them living long lives as they battled and clawed their way through decade after decade. But again, we need to look at the evidence before we decide anything.

The oldest *T. rex* we are aware of is that famous lady, Sue, who was only 28 years old when she died. We know this because, like the trunks of trees, some animals have growth rings on their bones, marking the amount of growth that individual managed over a year. The spacing between each of these rings tells us how fast or slow that growth was. If the rings are far apart, then the animal grew quickly. If they are close, then growth had slowed, or stopped. When the rings are really close, they are bones from an adult.

By looking at the high number of well-preserved bones discovered in the last ten years or so, and the ring patterns on them, it has been possible to show that *T. rex* grew very quickly until it reached adulthood in its late teens. It stopped growing at around 19 years of age. Their

Although they would grow up to be one of the largest and most successful land predators ever, *T. rex* babies were vulnerable to predators. In order to avoid being eaten by a hungry *Quetzalcoatlus*, *T. rex* juveniles grew fast, putting on about 2kg in weight a day.

bones tell a fascinating story. For an incredible four-year period, these developing animals impressively put on more than 2kg per day. Until we have more evidence to suggest they lived longer lives, it appears the most famous of the predatory dinosaurs grew up fast and died young.

CLASSIFICATION

If you want to learn everything there is to know about a single species, it helps to look at the other species that are closely related. Looking at the family tree of a species or a group of species is called taxonomy (tax-on O-ME) and understanding the classification from a scientific perspective allows us to explore evolutionary relationships, behaviour and the role the organism played, or plays, within its environment. So, what does the *Tyrannosaurus rex* family tree look like?

The theropods were the well-known, two-legged carnivorous dinosaurs, and the group included *T. rex* (and its cousins), *Spinosaurus* (SPY-no sor-us), *Allosaurus* (allo sor-us), *Giganotosaurus* (gig-a NO-TOE sor-us),

Tyrannosauridae

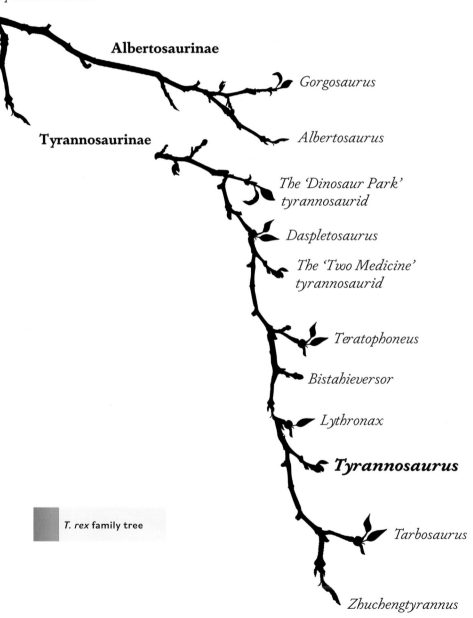

Albertosaurinae

Gorgosaurus

Albertosaurus

Tyrannosaurinae

The 'Dinosaur Park' tyrannosaurid

Daspletosaurus

The 'Two Medicine' tyrannosaurid

Teratophoneus

Bistahieversor

Lythronax

Tyrannosaurus

Tarbosaurus

Zhuchengtyrannus

T. rex family tree

Guanlong

Yutyrannus

Alioramus

Albertosaurus

Daspletosaurus

Tarbosaurus

Velociraptor (vel oss-EE rap-tor), *Microraptor* (MY-cro rap-tor), *Oviraptor* (ov-EE rap-tor), *Therizinosaurus* (th-er iz-in O-sor-us) and even the birds we see today. Within the theropods was a smaller group called Coelurosauria (SEEL-ur O-sor-EE-a) and it's in *this* group that we find the Tyrannosauridae (TY ran O-sor i-DAY) – which included *T. rex* and its closest relatives.

What: *Tarbosaurus* (tar-bo-sor-us)
Name meaning: 'alarming lizard'
When/where: 70 million years ago in Asia
Size: 12m long, 4.5 tonnes (same as a big African elephant)
Did you know? It had the smallest arms of all tyrannosaurids

What: *Albertosaurus*
Name meaning: 'Alberta lizard'
When/where: 70 million years ago in Canada
Size: 9m long, 2 tonnes (same as a family car)
Did you know? It was a pack hunter – fossils from 26 animals were found at the Dry Island bonebed site

What: *Daspletosaurus* (daz-plet-O sor-us)
Name meaning: 'frightful lizard'
When/where: Between 77 and 74 million years ago in North America
Size: 9m long, could weigh almost 4 tonnes
Did you know? It had the longest forelimbs of any tyrannosaurid

The tyrannosaurids have two parts to their family – the Albertosaurs (al-bert O-sorz) and the tyrannosaurs. Scientists think there may have been about 11 different branches on the Tyrannosauridae tree but some believe there might only have been three. The truth is that we don't know yet and *T. rex* is just a branch in a much more complex family tree.

All of the tyrannosaurids were big, two-legged carnivores, with huge, broad skulls and large teeth. They had long legs and were fast for their size but their arms were small and they usually only had two digits (fingers). Fossils of tyrannosaurids have been found in North America and Asia and when alive, these animals were nearly always the biggest predators in their ecosystems.

ECOLOGY

In brand new research scientists have predicted there may have been as many as 2.5 billion *T. rex* during their existence. That means over 20,000 were alive at any one time at the end of the Cretaceous.

To fully understand *Tyrannosaurus rex*, we need to look at its environment, the other species (animals, plants, fungi and other organisms within that environment, the role *T. rex* played and the relationship it had with every other part of that ecosystem. The role of a species within its environment and the relationship it has with every other part of its ecosystem is known as its ecology. In many ways, the ecology of *T. rex* is pretty simple to understand. It was mostly a one-way relationship in that *T. rex* was a predator and preyed on other species.

As *T. rex* had a wide distribution across Laramidia (la-ra mid-EE-a), the long, thin, ancient island continent which forms part of the USA today, they would have been found in different habitats. It appears

There is still much to learn about the social behaviour and hunting techniques of *T. rex*. The death of a large animal often brings predators together even if they are not usually social. This dead *Alamosaurus* has attracted a group of *T. rex*, which will feast here for months.

T. rex would have ranged from Canada in the north to as far south as New Mexico. *T. rex* would have existed, 66 million years ago, in desert-like plains, subtropical coastal habitats and inland, slow-flowing swampy environments, similar to the American everglades today. Overall, the environment was said to be subtropical, with a humid, warm climate. In the northern portion of its range, *T. rex* would have encountered *Triceratops* as the most common herbivore, while the large titanosaur *Alamosaurus* (allamo sor-us) dominated the southern part of their range.

When

The Cretaceous period was the last of the three geological stages made famous by the dinosaurs and it stretched between 145 million and 66 million years ago. Fossilised bones from *Tyrannosaurus rex* have been dated from between 68 million and 66 million years ago, showing that *T. rex* lived right at the end of the Cretaceous period and was one of the last dinosaurs around before the asteroid struck.

This is how the Earth looked at the end of the Cretaceous period.

Where

From fossil discoveries, it appears *Tyrannosaurus rex* had a much wider range than other members of the tyrannosaur group. They were restricted to the ancient island continent Laramidia, which now forms part of the North American continent. Fossils are restricted to western parts of North America, in an area known as the Hell Creek Formation, across Montana, South Dakota, North Dakota and Wyoming in the USA, and in Alberta and Saskatchewan in Canada.

Environment

The greatest of the ancient land masses was Pangaea (pan JEE-a), a supercontinent that formed around 335 million years ago and dominated the planet, before starting to break up around 160 million years later. The *smaller* parts would go on to become the continents we know today, although they looked different then. The breakup of Pangaea started during the Jurassic and continues to this day, though its separation was mostly complete by the end of the Cretaceous period. Throughout most of the period, North America was two separate blocks of land, separated by a narrow, shallow sea. The western land mass was called Laramidia and Appalachia (ap-a LAY-SHE-a) sat to the east.

Over the course of the Cretaceous, the climate warmed up, so that by the time *T. rex* was stalking Laramidia, the temperature was between 21 and 23°C, in the location which is now western Texas. If you take an average temperature across the whole of the Cretaceous period, the Earth was about 4°C warmer than it is today, but looking specifically at Laramidia at the time when *T. rex* was alive, the average temperature was 22°C, which is almost the same as the average for western Texas now.

Unlike today, when there is a large range of temperature between the tropical, hot equator and either of the freezing cold poles, temperature across the planet was more even in the Cretaceous. Without the range in temperature, there would have been weaker winds and, because of that, weaker ocean currents. The Earth's oceans would have been more stagnant during the late Cretaceous, making it difficult for life as the surface water temperature in tropical seas may have reached an almost unbelievable 42°C, 17°C warmer than they are today.

This *Tyrannosaurus rex* tries to panic a huge herd of *Edmontosaurus*, to separate any weaker, older or younger animals.

Flora and fauna

Just imagine a hungry *Tyrannosaurus rex* stalking the prehistoric landscape, scanning the horizon for food. That seems a simplistic view and may be unfair, because *T. rex* would have been so much more than an eating machine, but it's a safe guess that every other animal alive would have been thinking the same. Although there may have been bigger predatory dinosaurs, *T. rex* was the biggest

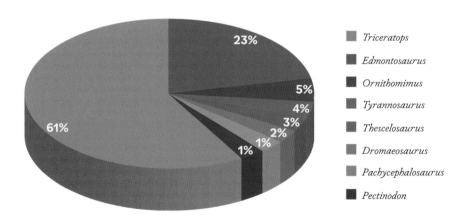

A breakdown of the most commonly found dinosaur fossils in the Hell Creek Formation.

predator within its environment. Fossil finds have shown that the Hell Creek Formation was rich in biodiversity, with a host of plants and animals.

Having a more complete understanding of the flora and fauna found in the same area as a particular species helps us understand that species in greater detail. Fossil discoveries have shown the most common dinosaur in the area before the asteroid struck was *Triceratops*. One of the most easily recognisable dinosaurs, this huge herbivore had three distinct horns, each up to a metre in length. Measuring up to 9m long and weighing as much as 12 tonnes, young and very old *Triceratops* would have been likely *T. rex* prey.

Other large herbivores, such as the large 'duck-billed' *Edmontosaurus* (ed mon-tow sore-us), were also present. These hadrosaurs grew up to 15m in length, may have weighed over 9 tonnes and lived in groups of as many as 20,000 individuals.

A pack of dakotaraptors harass a much larger *Tyrannosaurus rex* in a dangerous attempt draw her away from a kill. Although *T. rex* was the largest predator within its environment, other species of theropods lived alongside it.

Smaller predators, such as the *Troodon* relative *Pectinodon* (pek-tin O-don) as well as the fast-running, feathered *Ornithomimus* (orn ith-O MY-muss), were also in the area, along with the truly formidable *Ankylosaurus* (ank-EE LO-sor-us), with its low centre of gravity, rows of spines and bony armour, and a huge clubbed tail to defend itself.

Much of the Hell Creek Formation was dominated by low-lying habitat where the ground was wet, and many of the trees found there would be the same as today. Thick woodlands would have been full of sycamores, beech, laurels and magnolias. Fossils from palm trees and evergreen conifers have also been found, with a range of mosses and ferns.

Behaviour

There is a myth that dinosaurs were dumb, and, before we knew about *that* asteroid, some people thought they may have gone extinct because they simply weren't clever enough to survive, which is not only bonkers but wrong. It's likely that *Tyrannosaurus rex* was much smarter than you might imagine and had highly tuned senses, which would have taken a good chunk of brain power and mental processing.

There's always a temptation to ask how clever a particular animal might be and it's a difficult question. You might think you're more intelligent than a chimpanzee but trust me, if you were both left in a tropical forest for a week, I know which of you would be able to find food, water, shelter and avoid predators. When looking at how intelligent *T. rex* might have been, there is still disagreement. Until we know more for certain, it's tempting to imagine the *T. rex* as an intelligent hunter with a range of finely tuned sensory adaptations.

From looking at the skull, it appears *T. rex* had, in comparison to the size of its brain, large olfactory bulbs sitting near the front of the brain. These bulbs are structures made from nervous tissue, stretching from the brain and extending into the roof of the nasal cavity. They help translate smells into electrical messages which are processed in the brain. In *T. rex*, such large olfactory bulbs mean it had a highly developed sense of smell, which may have helped it hunt prey or scavenge by smelling carcasses long distances away. Research has shown that of all the dinosaurs studied, *T. rex* had the most highly developed sense of smell.

It also had a good sense of hearing. Compared to most other theropod dinosaurs, *T. rex* had unusually long cochlea (kok-LEE a). These are structures in the inner ear which look like whirlpools or snail shells. They receive vibrations made by sounds and help convert them into electrical signals which are processed in the brain. Longer cochlea means better hearing.

In a slightly related area, many of us want to know about what noises dinosaurs made, if they made any at all. We have all watched cartoons and blockbuster films with roaring dinosaurs but, as scientists, we need to look at the evidence before we can be certain. There is some discussion around the idea that because they are closely related, maybe dinosaurs made very low rumbling sounds like alligators and their

relatives. Others have focused on what we can (and can't) find in the fossil record.

We usually call them voice boxes but the proper name for the anatomy in our throat responsible for making noises is called the larynx (la-rinks). Nearly every terrestrial vertebrate vocalises in this way, but not the birds. They use a slightly different structure called the syrinx (si-rinks). The syrinx sits much further down the windpipe than a larynx does, and can be found just where the lungs branch off. It's worth remembering that while not all larynxes are used to vocalise, syrinxes are *only* used to make sounds. In 2016, a 66-million-year-old fossil syrinx was found in Antarctica, showing that these structures were around at the same time as *T. rex*, although so far, no syrinxes have been found for non-avian dinosaurs. This may mean that non-avian dinosaurs such as *T. rex* and its relatives didn't possess syrinxes and did not communicate as birds do today, or it could just be that we haven't found any of these fragile fossils yet.

One other possibility is that dinosaurs made hissing sounds, like vultures, or boomed, like ostriches, both of which are examples of birds that don't have syrinxes. As for what sound that very old Antarctic syrinx fossil would have made, research shows it most likely made a honking sound, like a goose, so unless you are willing to accept that *T. rex* honked like a supersized goose, it's safe to say they did not roar like a Hollywood *T. rex* either.

After knowing what senses they used for hunting, the next question is what their hunting behaviour was like. Did they hunt alone or in groups? Did they just hunt or did they scavenge too? Some researchers have suggested *T. rex* may have been social hunters, forming packs to capture their prey. While this is a fascinating idea, there isn't any evidence for group hunting in *T. rex* so far. Similarly, the idea that *T. rex* were scavengers is one that won't go away. Many of nature's most amazing predators, such as polar bears, great white sharks and golden eagles, practise scavenging at some level. Nobody is saying that *T. rex* didn't scavenge to some degree, but some scientists have argued that *T. rex only* scavenged and wasn't able to hunt. Again, there is no evidence for this, so *T. rex* remains the greatest predator of all time.

T. rex's bite was more powerful than any other land animal ever. Some estimates put their bite force at between 35,000 and 57,000 Newtons (N), which is a unit for measuring force. If you want to get a sense of how much that is, hyenas have a world-famous bite and generate 2,000N. A great white shark has a bite force of around 18,000N. Yours? When you're fully grown, you should be able to generate a maximum bite force of around 890N. The bite force of *T. rex* was 50 times greater than that of an adult human. Part of this colossal force was achieved by their ability to open their mouth to an angle of around 80 degrees, helping power that impressive bite. Once an unfortunate animal was caught between their jaws, it's likely *T. rex* tore them apart by shaking its head from side to side, like crocodiles do today.

One of the most interesting things about *T. rex* behaviour is how they behaved with one another, and although we don't know whether they happily hunted together or moved around in packs, we do know they did interact and that it didn't always end well. Some of the most famous *T. rex* discoveries, such as Stan and Scotty, have broken and healed ribs, fractured and healed vertebrae, and both show healed holes on the skull that look a lot like puncture marks from the teeth of another *T. rex* during a fight.

Finally, and in a weird twist, it appears that the mightiest of the dinosaurs had one dangerous enemy (other than unexpected asteroids), and the fossil bones of some tell how the largest can be brought down by the smallest. Fifteen per cent of *T. rex* fossils, including Scotty and even Sue, show signs of an infection called trichomoniasis (trik-O mon-I-ass-iss), caused by

Biggest isn't always best. Here, a once-mighty predator is thin and weak, suffering from the effects of an infection by microscopic parasites.

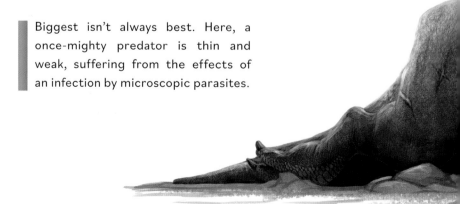

a microscopic parasite. Infected animals develop painful yellow lumps on their gums and around the mouth. As the infection worsens, smooth-edged holes and pits, usually on and around the jaw, develop. Some of the affected *T. rex* bones show holes several centimetres in diameter and it is thought some animals had so many that the jaw itself became eroded and weakened. This same parasitic infection is common in many species of birds today, especially raptors. In *T. rex*, the infection spread from one animal to another either from fighting, cannibalism or from eating infected prey, although evidence of similar infection has never been found in fossils from herbivorous dinosaurs. Some of the infections found in *T. rex* fossils were so bad, and likely caused such severe pain, that they starved to death.

GLOSSARY

Bipedal (BI PEE-dal)
The behaviour of walking on two legs. Birds (and other theropod dinosaurs), kangaroos and humans are examples of bipedal animals.

Equator (EE-KWAY tor)
This imaginary line runs around the centre of the Earth and passes through the tropics. It is halfway between the North and South poles and is also known as zero degrees latitude.

Extant
If a species, or group of species, still exists, it is said to be extant.

Extinct
If a species, or group of species, no longer exists, it is said to be extinct. If so few are left that they can no longer breed,

even though some are alive, then the species, or group, is known as being *functionally* extinct.

Laramidia (laar-a mid-EE-a)
A long, thin, ancient island continent which formed over 90 million years ago, during the late Cretaceous period, when rising seas flooded the middle of North America and split it in two. Today, Laramidia is buried under the western parts of the USA.

Pangaea (pan JEE-a)
A supercontinent that existed during the late Palaeozoic and early Mesozoic eras. It was made from previous supercontinent material and formed approximately 335 million years ago. It started to break apart around 175 million years ago.

Serrated
A sharp, jagged edge, like a saw.

Terrestrial (ter-ess TREE-al)
On the land.

Titanosaur (TIE-tan O-sor)
A group of herbivorous dinosaurs within the wider group known as the titanosaurs. These were the largest

dinosaurs ever and included animals such as *Patagotitan*, *Dreadnoughtus* and *Argentinosaurus*. The biggest of these weighed over 75 tonnes.

Tyrannosaurids (TIE-ranno sor-idz)
A group within the larger group of theropod dinosaurs. The tyrannosaurids includes the albertosaurs and the more famous tyrannosaurs, including *Tyrannosaurus rex*.

Vertebrae (vur-ter BRAY)
The back bones in a vertebrate skeleton. Lots of vertebrae together make up the spinal column.

Collect all eight titles in the E✗TINCT series

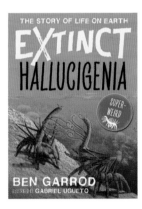

One of the oldest and most mysterious animals ever described, *Hallucigenia* was a kind of sea-living, armoured worm. But it was nothing like the worms we know today. Its body was covered in spines and frills. It had claws at the end of its legs and a mouth lined with sharp teeth.

This strange animal was one of the victims of the End Ordovician mass extinction which claimed 85 per cent of the species living in the world's oceans around 443 million years ago. What could have led to this catastrophe and what caused the appearance of huge glaciers and falling sea levels, leaving many marine ecosystems dry and unable to sustain life at a time when it had only just got started?

An armoured fish with a bite 10 times more powerful than that of a great white shark, *Dunkleosteus* could also snap its jaws five times faster than you can blink! It was one of the most iconic predators ever to rule the waves. What was it like to live in its shadow? And how did it become one of the many victims of the Late Devonian mass extinction around 375 million years ago?

Let's discover why this mass extinction only affected ocean life and why it went on for so long – some scientists believe it lasted for 25 million years. In a weird twist, we'll look at whether the evolution of trees on the land at that time was partly responsible for the loss of so many marine species, including *Dunkleosteus*.

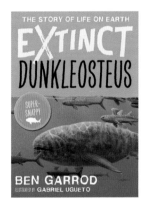

Among the first arthropods - animals with jointed legs such as insects and their relatives - trilobites were around on Earth for over 300 million years and survived the first two mass extinctions. There were once at least 20,000 species but all disappeared in the devastating End Permian mass extinction around 252 million years ago.

We'll look at why land animals were affected this time as well as those in the sea. An incredible 96 per cent of marine species went extinct and an almost equally terrible 70 per cent of life on land was wiped out in what is known as the *Great Dying*. This was the closest we've come to losing all life on Earth and the planet was changed forever.

At a massive 9 tonnes, the elephant-sized *Lisowicia* was one of the largest animals on the planet during the Late Triassic. A kind of cross between a mammal and a reptile but not quite either, *Lisowicia* was a distant cousin of the ancient mammals - and they eventually led to our very own ancestors.

We'll discover why the End Triassic mass extinction happened, changing the global environment and making life impossible for around 75 per cent of species. And how, while this fourth mass extinction may have been devastating for most life on Earth, it gave one group of animals - dinosaurs - the chance to dominate the planet for millions of years.

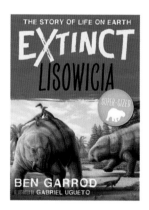

A giant marine predator, megalodon grew up to an incredible 18m - longer than three great white sharks, nose to tail. This ferocious monster had the most powerful bite force ever measured. It specialised in killing whales by attacking them from the side, aiming for their heart and lungs.

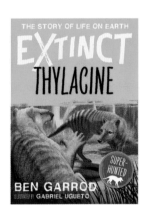

But, like more than 50 per cent of marine mammals and many other creatures, megalodon disappeared in the End Pliocene mass extinction around 2.5 million years ago. We'll find out why this event affected many of the bigger animals in the marine environment and had an especially bad impact on both warm-blooded animals and predators.

The thylacine, also known as the Tasmanian tiger, is one of a long list of species, ranging from sabre-toothed cats to the dodo, that have been wiped out by humans. The last wild thylacine was shot in 1930 and the last captive thylacine alive died in a zoo in 1936.

We'll explore the mass extinction we are now entering and how we, as a species, have the power to wipe out other species - something no other single species is able to do. Who are the winners and losers and why might it take over seven million years to restore mammal diversity on Earth to what it was before humans arrived?

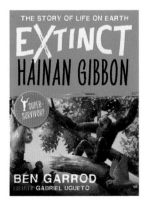

One of the most endangered animals on our planet, the Hainan gibbon is also one of our closest living relatives. Family groups of these little primates live in the trees on an island off the south coast of China and they feed on leaves and fruit.

But the gibbons are now in serious trouble because of the effects of human population increase around the world and habitat destruction. Without action, this animal might soon be extinct and need a dagger after its name. What can we all do to help stop some of our most interesting, iconic and important species from going extinct?

BEN GARROD is Professor of Evolutionary Biology and Science Engagement at the University of East Anglia. Ben has lived and worked all around the world, alongside chimpanzees in Africa, polar bears in the Arctic and giant dinosaur fossils in South America. He is currently based in the West Country. He broadcasts regularly on TV and radio and is a trustee and ambassador of a number of key conservation organisations. His eight book series *Ultimate Dinosaurs* and *The Chimpanzee and Me* are also published by Zephyr.

GABRIEL UGUETO is a scientific illustrator, palaeoartist and herpetologist based in Florida. For several years, he was an independent herpetologist researcher and authored papers on new species of neotropical lizards and various taxonomic revisions. As an illustrator, his work reflects the latest scientific hypotheses about the external appearance and the behaviour of the animals, both extinct and extant, that he reconstructs. His illustrations have appeared in books, journals, magazines, museum exhibitions and television documentaries.

Zephyr is an imprint of Head of Zeus.
At Zephyr we are proud to publish books
you can read and re-read time and time
again because they tell a brilliant story
and because they entertain you.

[t] @_ZephyrBooks

[instagram] @_zephyrbooks

[f] HeadofZeusBooks

readzephyr.com

www.headofzeus.com

ZEPHYR